How to Start and Sustain a Faith-Based SMALL GROUP

How to Start and Sustain a Faith-Based SMALL GROUP

John D. Schroeder

ABINGDON PRESS / NASHVILLE

HOW TO START AND SUSTAIN A FAITH-BASED SMALL GROUP

Copyright © 2002 by Abingdon Press

This book is printed on acid-free, elemental-chlorine–free paper.

Library of Congress Cataloging-in-Publication Data

Schroeder, John D.
    How to start and sustain a faith-based small group / John D. Schroeder.
        p. cm. — (How to start—)
    ISBN 0-687-08002-9 (pbk.: alk. paper)
    1. Church group work.   2. Small groups—Religious aspects—Christianity.   I. Title.   II. Series.
    BV652.2 .S37 2002
    253'.7—dc21

                                                            2002007269

02 03 04 05 06 07 08 09 10 11—10 9 8 7 6 5 4 3 2 1

MANUFACTURED IN THE UNITED STATES OF AMERICA

CONTENTS

INTRODUCTION

God cares for people through people. It's been that way throughout the ages. The Bible is full of examples of how God has used people to minister to others. God sometimes comes in the form of a friend, brother, sister, father, mother, or even a stranger to help in time of need. People are God's hands, feet, and voice in our world.

People helping people grow in faith is the ministry of the small group. A small group is usually a group of twelve or fewer who gather together on a regular basis to study God's word and encourage one another in the faith. It is people ministering to one another. As Jesus used his twelve disciples to change the world, God can use small groups to change lives.

Just like people, all small groups are unique. No two are exactly alike. Every group will have different perspectives, dynamics, feelings, and adventures. Conversations will range from secular to spiritual, humorous to serious, and will cover various aspects of the Christian faith. Each session will be different as participants share their faith, struggles, questions, and concerns.

Small groups provide an opportunity for individuals to discuss issues of faith in a nonthreatening and supportive environment. It is Christians talking with Christians, friends talking with friends, and God speaking to us through others and through the Bible. Small group members learn from one another as ideas and experiences are shared.

Love and acceptance are important aspects of each small group. All members are accepted just as they are. People will participate in the group having varying experience in the faith, from seekers to beginning believers all the way to those strong in the faith. And each has something to contribute that is of value to each of the others.

Likewise, people will come to the group with different needs and expectations. Each person will be at a different point on life's journey, but all will be heading toward the same destination. It is the function of the small group to assist each one on this journey, to answer questions, to give directions, to offer support and love. No one travels alone in a small group.

This book is intended to be a road map for your

journey, from conception to completion. Like human beings, small groups are life forms that are born, flourish, and eventually die. This book contains options and information on which road to take. There are many roads that reach the same destination. As you begin your journey, there are many decisions to be made. This guide contains ideas and information about how to begin. Use the ideas that you think will work best for you. Feel free to experiment.

Finally, since you are starting a faith-based small group, use prayer to guide you and your group toward the destination God has in mind for you. The journey will be one like you have never had before, and God will be with you every step of the way.

CHAPTER 1

Initial Decisions, Options, and Planning

Congratulations! You are about to experience the birth of a small group, a ready-made family of individuals who will touch the lives of one another. As a leader and organizer, you will need to make some decisions and do some planning in order to achieve your objectives. Let's begin with your objectives.

✳ Decisions About Goals

Why do you want to form a small group? Consider what you want to accomplish. You might wish to start by making two lists. The first list could be goals or outcomes for the group and individuals involved. How will participants become more effective Christians as a result of this small group? What do you desire for long-term results and objectives? More biblical knowledge? Better listeners? Increased ability to witness?

Here are some possibilities of a focus for a small group:

- Learning more about the book of Revelation
- Being better able to minister to young adults
- Becoming closer to Jesus
- Ministering to peers within the church
- Gaining spiritual maturity
- Effective daily living as a Christian
- Witnessing to others
- Learning your identity as a Christian
- Discovering the power of the Lord's Prayer
- Learning more about Christ's twelve disciples
- Living a life of faith in a secular world

The number of topics has no limit. Since you are interested in starting a small group, you probably already have an idea about the topic and focus for the group. If you want some more ideas, visit your local Christian bookstore. Chances are there will be some book focusing on your small group study, whether it is the Bible or a book on a specific topic by a Christian author. Consider your many options!

A second list could focus on meeting the needs of the individuals who will become members of the small group. The question is: What needs will be met by participating in this group? **It is important**

to remember that people join groups in order to have their needs met. They come to the group for a reason and with an agenda. Participants will also have different needs from each other. One person may join solely for friendship (to make new Christian friends) while others may want to jump-start their prayer life. A small group can satisfy multiple needs, but these needs should be considered in your initial planning.

✶ Decisions About Participants

Once you have some idea why you want to form a small group and have decided on a focus and needs that can be met, it is time to think about your prospective participants. The first decision is the number of participants.

How small or large is a small group? There are several factors to consider in determining how many people to include in your group. You will want the number to be small enough so everyone gets a chance to participate. That's the main rule. Groups can be as small as three or four people, or as large as twelve people. Usually limiting the group to six to ten members is best. Remember that some people will be absent from time to time. You also want to take into account the size and seating in the room. Are the participants gathered around a table, or are they seated in a living room? People need to be comfortable and able to hear each other.

The type of people is another consideration. Is your small group going to be composed of young adults, seniors, only men, only women, singles, married, teens, people from only your church, people from the neighborhood, people from work, or anyone who wants to attend?

Your topic or focus for the group may play a role in deciding the type of participants. If the topic is geared toward men or toward women, a same gender group may be your best option, although members of the opposite sex can give a group a valuable perspective. A men's Bible study is a common small group in many churches. Many churches have circles of small groups just for women.

Sometimes it is good if everyone has something in common. Groups with all teens or all seniors give participants a common basis from which to begin discussions. Teens relate well to other teens. Seniors relate well to other seniors. It doesn't have to be this way, however. Mixed groups of married, single, teens, seniors, and those within and outside of the church can give the group valuable insights as each one shares from his or her own perspective and life experience.

The question comes down to whether you want a group with the same or different perspectives and life experiences. Once this is decided, gear the topic to the type of people in the small group.

✶ Length of Meetings

In preparation for launching your small group, you also need to consider a number of aspects about your meetings. Over how many weeks or months will your small group continue to meet? How long will each session last? What is the best night or day to have sessions? Will you meet once a week or every other week? What will be the best starting time?

One option is to have a "permanent" small group that goes on week after week, month after month. A ten-week study of Acts might be followed by a study of evangelism for six weeks. As the topics change, the number of participants would change as people opt in or opt out, depending on personal interests and schedules. Leaders could also change with the topics. A core group of participants might remain from topic to topic with the addition of some new people to add interest and variety to the group.

You could also have a seasonal small group that runs four times a year: spring, summer, autumn, and winter. Participants and topics could change with the seasons.

Another idea is to have an "open" small group with

a different topic each time. Anyone could show up and join the discussion. You might have a core group with a new person once in a while, and people could bring a friend. An attractive option would be not having any strict attendance requirements; people would attend as they are able. It would be known that your church has a small group with changing topics that meets, for example, each Tuesday at 7 P.M. for ninety minutes, and all are welcome.

In most cases, the number of times your small group will meet will be decided by your choice of topic and material. Once a week or twice a month is common for most small groups. If the book you selected has twelve chapters, that pretty much determines the number of meetings.

The length of each session for many small groups is from one hour to ninety minutes. You want to allow enough time for social time, topic discussion, and perhaps an activity. Most participants find they can spare an hour a week, plus travel time to and from the discussion location. You want to allow enough time to accomplish your session goals while respecting individual time restrictions.

✶ Selecting Your Material

When it comes to discussion material for your small group, there are thousands of options. You may already know exactly the text you want to use, and if so, you can move on to other decisions. If you are undecided, two options are using your Bible or using a book with a Christian theme for your discussion. Your local Christian bookstore or your church library can provide many ideas and options. You can also use the Internet to explore potential material.

If you are planning a small group Bible study, there are a few things to keep in mind. All participants should be using the same version of the Bible. The leader should determine the version, perhaps with input from participants. You could ask what version they own and go with the majority, if you desire. Or your group may find that the use of different versions can add additional perspective to understanding a passage.

Your local bookstore is an excellent source for locating discussion guides for various books of the Bible. Discussion guides contain questions for the group to answer and sometimes group activities. Your first step is to select which book of the Bible you want to study. Discussion guides exist for most books. You will want to select a guide that is compatible with your beliefs and your denomination. Compare the number of weeks or sessions in the guide, and compare costs. You also need to decide if you want to purchase just one study guide for the leader, or if you want each member to have a guide and access to the weekly questions. Your pastor may also have suggestions on which study guide to use.

If you want to use a book with a Christian theme, there are thousands to choose from. Again, your church library and your local Christian bookstore are great places to begin your search. Many Christian publishers, such as Abingdon Press, are now including a built-in study guide in the back of many books. Separate companion study guides for Christian books are also available from many publishers. Many books are located in the Inspirational or Christian Living sections of bookstores. Again, your pastor may be able to suggest a book.

Of course, not all books come with a study guide containing questions for a group discussion. Having a ready-made study guide does make it easier for the discussion leader, but you can lead a discussion without a leader guide. In such a case, the leader and/or the participants would be responsible for the questions.

Another option is to study a secular book and focus on how it relates to your Christian faith. For example, a book on job hunting could be used for a small group of participants who are unemployed. Topics for each session could include prayer, networking with other Christians, contacts within the church, trusting in God, and other related themes. Another example is a secular book on gardening with homemade questions on spiritual themes such as faith, spiritual nourishment, and planting seeds. Verses from the Bible could serve as themes.

Note that selection of a book and topic does not have to be done alone. You could go to a Christian bookstore with two or three members of your future group and select a text you want to study. Another alternative is to select a topic, then bring several book choices to your first meeting and let the participants decide. Generally it does work better if you have the book selected before your first meeting.

Take care in selecting a book. Your choice can affect the quality of the discussions. What you want to look for in a book is a subject that would hold the interest of your small group for a month or two. You may want to read the book in its entirety before the group starts to determine if you can live with it for several months. Consider whether the text would encourage good discussion. Is it suited for the age level of your group? Does it contain stories that illustrate Christian themes? Is it easy to read or quite dry? And finally, ask yourself if this is a book that is worth the time that will be invested. Consider whether your participants will gain spiritual growth and insights as a result of reading this book.

Remember that the book you select is a catalyst for God to work within your group. Much of the spiritual growth may come from the discussions and members ministering to one another.

✴ Your Small Group Budget

It doesn't take much money to launch a small group. Normally, the cost of the book is picked up by each of the participants. You might want to determine whether your church can pay for the initial cost of the books, then be reimbursed by the group participants after the group begins meeting. Sometimes if the church purchases the books, there may be a discount. If members are using their own Bibles for the discussion, you could have a small group with no financial cost for anyone.

You may want to budget for promoting the group with flyers and registration forms. Weekly snacks could be the responsibility of each group member on a rotating basis. Before your small group is launched, you may want to consider the cost of any field trips that your group may take. If the book you have selected is expensive, you might determine whether your church could pay part of the cost or pay for books for members who can't afford them.

✴ Decisions About Leadership

Chances are that if you are reading this book, you intend to lead the group. There are other leadership options, however. Leadership can be shared by coleaders or can rotate from week to week.

Group leadership involves a number of responsibilities. Beyond the tasks involved in starting the group, a leader is the facilitator at each meeting, asking the questions and moving the discussion along. The leader also keeps track of individual members. Members call the leader if they are unable to attend. The leader is responsible for notifying members if the meeting is canceled. Some responsibilities can be delegated. The leader is the shepherd of the group, looking out for his or her flock. If problems develop within the group, the group leader deals with them. The leader is also responsible for lesson preparation each week and for planning for any after-discussion group activities or social events.

Additional leadership guidelines on how to lead a group discussion are in chapter 3.

As previously mentioned, the leader also decides where and when to meet. Normally, a small group meets at a church or at the homes of members. Other options are rooms in public libraries or in restaurants. The criteria for deciding on a location includes lighting, size of the group, comfortable seating, privacy, and closeness to the members' homes. Available parking and the safety of the area are also factors. The meeting room will need to be available for the length of the small group meetings without any scheduling conflicts with other groups.

CHAPTER 2

Promotion and Planning

After you have made the initial decisions, the next step is to publicize your small group and plan for your first meeting. You now know the book you will use, the day and time of the meeting, the location, and other considerations.

The first step is to attract members. There are several options. One of the easiest is word of mouth and personal invitation. Ask some friends and acquaintances if they would be interested in participating. Ask those who are interested if they know anyone else who would like to join the group.

Remember that the size of your group is limited, so you may want to begin with a goal of six, eight, or twelve people in mind. Once your goal is reached, keep a standby list for replacing those who are no-shows or cancellations. If you find yourself with twenty very interested candidates, consider recruiting a second leader and breaking into two groups.

Since having a small group means you are

dealing with a limited number of people, usually it is not difficult to find the six to twelve people you need. In recruiting your group, it is important to stress commitment to your potential members. You want people who will show up for each session during the coming weeks. Be aware that it is likely you may have one or more dropouts initially, so having some replacement members is a good idea.

If word of mouth doesn't attract enough members, other options include a notice in the church newsletter or Sunday bulletin. A poster on the church bulletin board is also a possibility.

✷ Information Gathering

This is where the record-keeping begins. Use a notebook or three-by-five index cards to record the names and phone numbers of those who make a commitment to join the group. Keep an additional list of people who have an interest, but for one reason or another are unable to attend. These are your backups. It is also important to give each person your name and telephone number so they can contact you should a problem arise.

It is at this point you probably want to collect money for purchasing books for each person. This solidifies commitment. Keep track in writing of who has paid for their book and who has not.

✫ Next Steps

Set a time, date, and location for your first meeting. This can be an introductory meeting, if you desire, where you get to know each other and you hand out the books. The next meeting would focus on the discussion of the first chapter. If members have the book in advance of the first meeting, book discussion could begin at the initial session.

It is a good idea for you to read the entire book in advance of the first meeting. This provides you with an overview and enables you to anticipate and answer questions that may arise.

It is better if other members read only one chapter per week and do not get ahead of the group. This helps focus the discussion on the chapter at hand. It also prevents one person from talking about something that another person may not have read yet. Communicate this to your members when you hand out the books.

Prior to the first meeting, create an outline of your first meeting with the amount of time you want to spend for each activity. Elements can include an opening social time and introductions, announcements, book discussion, an activity, prayer, and refreshments.

First meeting preparation also involves creating a checklist of what you want to bring to the initial meeting. This might include coffee, coffeemaker, refreshments, name tags, extra books, your Bible, extra pens and paper, along with anything else that you need.

You also might want to phone each member prior to the first meeting to remind them of the meeting and starting time. This provides an opportunity to get to know them a bit, and you can answer any questions they have.

CHAPTER 3

Small Group Meetings

You'll probably be both excited and nervous the day of your first small group meeting. You are about to begin a valuable ministry that can have an impact on individuals for years to come. Share your feelings with God in prayer and ask for guidance as you prepare to lead your first session.

Before you begin, remember that this first meeting will probably serve just two purposes. First, people will have time to get to know each other. Second, it will be a time for you to provide basic information to them and answer any questions. There may not be enough time for discussion of the first chapter of your book.

It's best to arrive early at the location of your small meeting so you can welcome all the participants and make introductions. Chances are you and your participants may not know everyone there. Try some icebreakers to help your members to mingle and become comfortable with one another.

☆ Icebreaker Ideas

- Give members a sheet of paper and pen as they enter. Ask them to get the autographs of all the other people.

- Have each person tell their favorite place; favorite person; and favorite pastime, recreation, or hobby. Since the first person sets the tone, choose someone who feels comfortable sharing with others. Encourage people to say as little or as much as they feel comfortable sharing with the group.

- For group introductions, have members give their entire name with the meaning and significance of their first and middle names. (Who were you named after?) As a second part of this process, members share their favorite fairy tale, explaining which character they relate to and why.

- As people enter the room, give each a card with the name of half a common pair written on it, for examples, Adam and Eve, Jack and Jill, salt and pepper. Ask each person to find the other half of the pair before the meeting starts.

- Break the group into pairs and have each person interview his or her partner for five minutes. Learn information such as name, family, occupation, and hobbies. After the interviews are completed, each person introduces his or her partner to the rest of the group.

- Ask participants to mingle and discover a common bond with each of the other people. It may be the same pair of shoes, being born in the same month or city, having graduated from the same school, and so forth. Have them report their common bonds prior to the discussion.

- Give all participants a paper and pencil, and have them form a circle. Give them two minutes to draw the face or profile of the person on their right. Have them write the name of the person on the back of the paper and give you the drawing. Later, you mix up the papers and have people try to pick out their own portrait.

Use your own imagination to think up other ways to help people start talking to each other. You may want to have an icebreaker at the start of both the first and second session.

✶ Getting Started

Depending on the size of your group, you may want to give each person a name tag for this first meeting.

After the icebreaker, ask your group to be seated. Welcome them. Share your enthusiasm for this opportunity to grow together in faith and to minister to one another. You may want to cover why this book was selected, give an overview of the book, and discuss what you want to accomplish as a small group. Ask participants to briefly talk about why they decided to participate and what they expect to receive and learn.

Review the format for each future meeting and tell how much time will be spent on each segment of the meeting:

1. social time as you wait for the meeting to begin

2. check-in, where members report how they are, what's new since last week, and so forth

3. announcements by the leader

4. book discussion, which can be followed by a group activity

5. closing prayer

6. refreshments, social time

✴ Establishing Guidelines

Explain that this small group is a family and has some ground rules for the benefit of the entire family. These rules include:

1. **Confidentiality.** What is said within the group stays within the group. Do not share personal information from this group with friends or family. This is a safe place to talk.

2. **Purpose.** This is not a therapy group, a sensitivity group, or an encounter group. We are here to grow in faith and to grow closer to God. We can offer Christian love and support to one another.

3. **Schedule.** Each session will start on time and end on time. Please be prompt. Let someone know if you will be unable to attend.

4. **Equality.** All are equal. No one is expected to be an expert on the topic.

5. **Acceptance.** It is important that each person be accepted by the rest of the group just as they are. We are all members of the family of God.

The leader or group should make a firm decision about whether the group will be open or closed. This decision creates guidelines for a group member wanting to bring a friend or family member to a future small group meeting. Normally, most short-term small groups are closed to new people, while long-term groups, ones that operate for several months, can be open to new people. Take into account the size of the group. You want it to remain small and manageable. It can also be difficult for both the new person and the group to adjust once a small group has been meeting for several weeks.

Recommend the following guidelines for your group.

1. What you receive from this study will be in direct proportion to your involvement. Feel free to share your thoughts about the material being discussed. Participate as your comfort level permits.

2. Please be supportive and encourage your fellow participants.

3. Please read the lesson and review the questions prior to the meeting. You may want to jot down answers to some of the questions.

4. You may have trouble or be unable to answer some discussion questions. This is not a problem. No one has all the answers, including your leader. Any ventured answer or guess is welcome.

5. Realize that all group members exercise leadership within a group. The health of your group's life belongs to all the group members, not the leader alone.

6. Give everyone a chance to participate in discussions. Back off from sharing your perspective if you sense you are dominating the discussion.

7. There may be more than one answer to some questions.

8. Please pray for your group and your leader.

Once you have reviewed the basics, you may or may not have time for discussion of the first lesson. If you have not done so already, you could distribute the books and talk about the book. This is also a good time to solicit questions from your group members. You could also end the meeting with more social time and/or another icebreaker.

✫ Discussion Suggestions

If you planned for and have time for discussion, go ahead. Here are some suggestions for facilitating the discussion:

1. Prior to the meeting, read the chapter and highlight important sentences or paragraphs. Make notes in the margins if you desire. Become comfortable with the material.

2. If your book contains questions or comes with a study guide that contains questions, review the questions in advance and jot down some notes if you desire. Remember, you don't have to use all the questions in the study guide. You can create your own.

3. If your book does not contain discussion questions, you can write your own. Jot down questions as they come to you while you read the lesson. You may want to begin group discussion with a general question each week,

such as "What new insights did you receive from reading this chapter?" You can also ask group members to begin the discussion with their own questions or a topic they want to discuss. (All the questions do not have to come from you.) You can write questions about the meaning of words. Ask members to talk about a personal experience with the topic of the session. One way to conclude discussion is by asking a general question such as "How has this discussion helped or challenged you?" Ask open-ended questions, ones that require more than a yes or no answer. Try to prepare about a dozen questions for each chapter.

4. For the first couple of sessions, you may want to begin by reminding participants that not everyone may feel comfortable reading aloud, answering questions, or participating in group discussion or activities. Let group members know that this is okay, and encourage them to participate as they feel comfortable doing so.

5. You could begin discussion by reviewing the main points of the chapter, providing the group with a summary. You may ask group members what they saw as highlights.

6. Encourage questions. Remind your participants that all questions are valid as part of the learning process. When you ask questions, you give permission for people to talk to others, exchanging thoughts and feelings.

7. Even if people don't talk during a discussion, you can be assured there is an internal dialogue enabling people to get in touch with their feelings.

8. Some questions may be more difficult to answer than others. If you ask a question and no one responds, begin the discussion by venturing an answer yourself. Then ask for comments and other answers. Remember that some questions have multiple answers.

9. Ask the question, "Why?" or "Why do you believe that?" to help continue a discussion and give it greater depth.

10. Allow silence. Sometimes, people need to think about something before they say anything. Recognize when the silence has gone on long enough. Some questions do fall flat. Some questions exhaust themselves. Some silence means that people really have

nothing more to say. With experience you'll learn to recognize different types of silence.

11. Give everyone a chance to talk. Keep the conversation moving. Occasionally you may want to direct a question at a specific person who has been quiet. "Do you have anything to add?" is a good follow-up question to ask. If the topic of conversation gets off track, move ahead by asking the next question.

12. Remember not to lecture your group. You are responsible for leading a discussion, not for conveying information.

13. Before moving from questions to something else, ask members if they have any questions that have not been answered.

14. Don't try to accomplish everything. Stick with your time limit. People become frustrated with group discussions that try to cover too much ground.

15. Remember that as a leader, you do not have to know all the answers. Some answers may come from group members. Other answers

may even need a bit of research. Your job is to keep the discussion moving and to encourage participation.

16. Be grateful and supportive. Thank members for their ideas and participation.

17. You are not expected to be a "perfect" leader. Just do the best you can by focusing on the participants and the lesson. God will help you lead this group.

18. Enjoy your time together.

✽ Group Activities

Discussion questions can be followed by a group activity. An activity is an excellent way to encourage group interaction, sharing of ideas and information. They can add depth to the topic being discussed. Here are some suggestions about planning an activity.

1. Some study guides include multiple suggestions for activities. This gives you the option of selecting which idea is best suited for your group. If you are not using a study guide, you or a group member can create your own

activity. You'll want to set aside a specific amount of time for this event.

2. Select your activity in advance and plan for it. If the activity requires pens and paper, be sure you bring them along. Create a checklist of all your activity requires. Drawing or creating something could be a group activity.

3. Your activity could be a group discussion on a specific topic or question. It might be creating a list of some sort related to your topic. If you come up with a hot question that lends itself toward a lengthy discussion, use it in the activity section of your meeting.

4. Your activity could be a movie or watching a video, followed by a brief group discussion.

5. Some groups use the Bible as a resource after completing discussion questions to delve into a specific aspect of a topic.

6. Magazines and newspapers are often used in an activity to search for local or national connections to the topic.

7. Try a field trip as an activity sometime over the course of your sessions. As an example, if

the topic is death or dying, a visit to a local cemetery or funeral home could be beneficial.

8. A practical application to what you are studying can become an excellent group activity. Visiting a nursing home as a group is a practical application for the topic of loneliness. Community service projects are also avenues to apply what you have been studying.

9. An activity could be a practical application after your meeting is over. It might be as simple as asking each member to share what they learned from this lesson with a family member or friend.

10. A challenge for the coming week could be an activity. For example, if the topic is kindness, the challenge could be to commit an act of kindness this week involving a total stranger. Members could report results at the next session.

✶ Group Prayer

After conclusion of the activity, it is appropriate to close in prayer. As leader, you can offer the prayer or ask for a volunteer. Here are some thoughts about praying in public:

- We pray to share how God is active in our lives today. Prayer in its simplest form is talking with God. It is not an occasion to impress others with how religious we are or how much we know about the Bible. Nor is prayer a platform to show how eloquently we speak. Prayer in its best form is an expression to God of our feelings, using words that come to us at the time.

- If you do not feel comfortable praying spontaneously, write down your prayer beforehand and simply read it out loud.

With this in mind—that the best prayer is a prayer from the heart—here are a few suggestions to quickly prepare for praying out loud:

1. Think of the occasion. How is the group feeling? What topic has just been discussed?

2. Are there any special requests important for those gathered together? Should a recent birth, an illness, or a death in the family be mentioned?

3. Be honest with your feelings. Are you joyful, worried, or unsure? Are you at a loss for words? People can relate to feelings more easily than theological jargon.

4. Be thankful. Even in death we are thankful for the gift and promise of eternal life. For what can you give God thanks? How has God been working in your midst?

5. Be brief. Keep your prayer short. People will appreciate your conservation of words.

Prayer options:

6. Ask people to bow their heads in a moment of silence. This way they can personalize their prayers and speak from their own hearts. You can simply end by saying something like, "Lord in heaven, hear our prayers."

7. Ask people in the group to each share one or two words that summarize their prayer to God at the moment. This is nonthreatening and lets the group be involved.

Like anything else, praying out loud becomes easier the more you do it. A good way to begin is to pray out loud when you are alone to get used to your voice and to become comfortable sharing your feelings publicly.

✶ Social Events

During the life of your small group, you may want to have a social event. This is an excellent opportunity for members to become better acquainted and to become more comfortable with each other. Social events can strengthen the bonds within a small group. The event does not need to cost much money and can be simple to organize.

Begin by selecting a date and time that is acceptable to all. Next, solicit suggestions from the group for an activity. Typical social events can be bowling, playing board games, going to a baseball or football game, going out to see a movie, watching a video at the home of a member—there are no shortages of activities. The problem may be deciding on one.

Once you have selected an activity, either the leader or a designated volunteer can handle the details. Transportation, refreshments, and costs can be shared or paid for individually. Maps may be needed for directions. Be sure to designate one person to call if a member has to cancel at the last minute.

CHAPTER 4

Sustaining Your Small Group

God does care for people through people. This is how your small group will be sustained, as people minister to one another. As leader, you can't sustain and nurture your small group alone. It is a group effort by you, your members, and God, working together.

First, remember that your small group is faith based. God uses your faith and the faith of your members to work within your small group. Prayer is one of the most important elements of sustaining a group. Your prayers, along with the prayers of your members, can work wonders in changing lives and drawing people closer to God. Prayer brings God in as an active participant in your small group. Pray for your group and encourage members to do the same. This will help sustain your group.

Second, remember the importance of being a good listener. Sometimes this involves listening to what is being said as well as what is not said. Listening can be just as vital to sustaining your group as words and actions. Listen for signs of people reaching out to others for help or for needs not being met. Keeping your ears open is an excellent way to keep an accurate pulse of your group and of individual members. Remind your participants of the importance of being good listeners.

Third, encourage members to minister to one another. This ministry can take many forms. It can be as simple as phoning someone during the week to see how he or she is or having a cup of coffee with a member after the meeting ends. Sharing your faith with one member or the entire group is a wonderful ministry. It all comes down to showing you care and putting your faith into action. Again, your small group is not a therapy group, and members need to understand the difference. However, showing love and concern for others is what God wants us to do, and this will sustain your small group.

Finally, remain receptive to God's spirit. God does work in mysterious ways to bring healing and to change lives. Seeds may be planted in your group that will blossom years later. Your group will be sustained by God, and you simply have to trust in that. You were all brought together by God for a purpose. Let God's spirit lead and sustain your ministry.

✳ Dealing with Problems

There may be bumps in the road in your journey. As in life, not everything goes the way you plan or would want it to be. You may need to adjust your original expectations or goals. God may be taking your group in another direction that is different from the path you intended to take. But what do you do if your group just does not seem to be working out?

First, figure out what is going on. Doing an evaluation may help. If you make the effort to observe and listen to your group, you may be able to anticipate and head off many potential problems.

Second, remember that the life span of your group is a relatively brief time, six to eight weeks normally. Most small groups will not have the chance to gel much in such a short period of time. Do not expect the kind of group development and nurture you might look for in a group that has lived and shared together for years.

Third, keep in mind that although you are a leader, the main responsibility for how the group develops belongs to the group itself. You do the best you can to create a hospitable setting for your group's interactions. You do your homework to keep the discussion and interactions flowing. But ultimately every member of the group individually and corporately bears responsibility for whatever happens within the life of the small group.

However, if any of these specific problems show up, try these suggestions:

If one member dominates the group, help the group identify this problem for itself by asking group members to rate or rank overall participation. In other words, have a discussion about how your discussions are going. Another option is to ask a discussion question with the request that each person respond briefly. As leader, you can also practice gate-keeping by saying, "We've heard from Joe; now what does someone else think?" If the problem becomes particularly troublesome, speak gently outside of a group session with the member who dominates.

If one member is reluctant to participate, ask each member to respond briefly to a discussion question in a round-robin fashion. Another option is to ask a reluctant participant what he or she thinks about the topic or question. You can also increase participation by dividing the larger group into smaller groups of two or three persons.

If the group chases rabbits instead of staying with the topic, judge whether the rabbit is really a legitimate or significant concern for the group to be discussing. By straying from your agenda, is the group setting an agenda more valid for their needs?

Another option is to simply restate the original topic or question. You could also ask yourself why the group seems to want to avoid a particular topic or question. If one individual keeps causing the group to stray inappropriately from the topic, speak to him or her outside of a session.

If someone drops out of the group, it might be because his or her needs are not being met within the group. You will never know this unless you ask that person directly. You could contact the person immediately following the first absence; otherwise, he or she is unlikely to return.

If the group or some members remain on a superficial level of discussion, this is not necessarily out of the ordinary. In a small group designed to last several weeks, you cannot necessarily expect enough trust to develop for a group to move deeper than a superficial level. Do not press an individual to disclose anything more than he or she is comfortable doing in the group. Encourage an atmosphere of confidentiality within the group. Whatever is said within the group stays within the group.

If someone shares a big, dangerous, or bizarre problem, remember your small group is not a therapy group. You should not take on the responsibility of "fixing" someone else's problem. You should encourage a member who shares a major problem to seek professional help. If necessary, remind the group about the need for confidentiality. If someone shares something that endangers either someone else or himself/herself, contact your pastor for advice.

✶ Making Changes

In order to sustain your small group, some changes may be in order. These changes may be small or large, depending on the needs of the group. You should consult the group before making any changes and solicit their opinions and ideas.

A common change is that the time or day of the meeting may need to be switched just for one time or for the remainder of the schedule to accommodate the needs of one or more people. Discuss this with all group members before coming to a decision.

For one reason or another, leadership may need to change. In this situation, the current leader should be honest with the group. Give the group time to adjust. A new leader could be selected through a volunteer process, or handpicked by the current leader. It is helpful if the new leader can be given some training or support from the old leader.

You may want to invite a special guest speaker to add depth to a particular topic. This guest could be a pastor or someone with specific knowledge of your topic. For example, if the topic for the session is death and dying, a hospice worker would be an appropriate guest. If you invite a guest speaker, it is helpful to brief the person about the format (question and answer or a short talk) and the amount of time involved. Inform your group in advance of the guest and let participants know whether they will be covering the scheduled lesson and questions.

✫ Evaluations

How do you know if your small group is healthy? In order to sustain your group, some regular evaluation is smart. As a leader, your observations which can often be based on your feelings are important. You should also evaluate with input from participants. You may want to evaluate your group after several meetings, rather than wait toward the end. Here are some ideas about how to evaluate the health of your small group.

Ask whether the group is measuring up to what the members expected of it. Go back to the first session where members said why they came to this small group. For an evaluation, you can ask members how well this experience measures up to their expectations.

Ask how members perceive group dynamics. Say: "On a scale from one to ten, with ten being the highest, where would you rate the overall participation by members of this group? On the same scale, where would you rate this group as meeting your needs? On the same scale, how would you rate the 'togetherness' of this small group?"

Ask group members to fill out an evaluation sheet on this small group experience. Keep the evaluation form simple. One of the simplest forms leaves plenty of blank space for responding to three requests: (1) Name the three things you would want to do more of. (2) Name the three things you want to do less of. (3) Name the three things you want to keep about the same.

Ask for direct feedback from one participant. Arrange ahead of time for a group member to stay a few minutes after a meeting or to meet with you the next day. Ask for direct feedback about what seemed to work or not work, who seems to be participating well, who seems to be dealing with something particularly troubling, and so forth.

Give group members permission to say when they sense something is not working. As the group leader, you do not hold responsibility for the life of the group. The group's life belongs to all the members of the group. Encourage group members to take responsibility for what takes place within the group session.

Expect and accept that, at times, discussions will fall flat, group interaction will be stilted, and

group members will be grumpy. All groups have bad days. Moreover, all groups go through their own life cycles. Although your six to twelve sessions may not be enough time for your small group to gel completely, you may find that after two or three sessions, one session will come when nothing seems to go right. That is normal. In fact, studies show that those groups that first show a little conflict begin to move into deeper levels of relationship.

Sit back and observe. In the middle of a discussion, sit back and try to look at the group as a whole. Does it look healthy to you? Is one person dominating? Does someone else seem to be withdrawn? How would you describe what you observe going on within the group at that time?

Take the temperature of the group. Try asking the group to take its own temperature. Would it be normal? Below normal? Feverish? What adjective would you use to describe the group's temperature?

Keep a record of evaluations. Try to use some form of evaluation several times during the life of the group. Compare evaluations to see how your group has changed.

☆ Ending Your Small Group Experience

There is a beginning and end to everything, including small groups. In most cases your group experience will end when the participants have covered all the chapters in the book you are studying. If the small group was scheduled to run for six, eight, or twelve weeks, the end will come as no surprise to the participants. Some will be ready to move on. Others will be sad and may have trouble letting go. Here are some suggestions on how to conclude your small group meetings.

Conclude the final discussion with some open-ended questions designed for closure. What was your favorite chapter and why? What did you learn about yourself or others from studying this book? How has participation in this small group changed you? Plan for a longer than normal discussion time. Close with a prayer giving thanks for the small group experience and the participants.

Plan a brief social time at the conclusion of the final session. Give participants a chance to mingle, chat, and say their farewells. Have some soft drinks and snacks available.

If ALL of the group approve, create a list of names and phone numbers so participants can keep in touch.

Thank the group members for their participation and for ministering to one another. Offer any observations you feel appropriate about the growth of your small group.

☆ Outside Resources

If you have a problem while leading the group, remember you can get advice from your pastor or from someone in your congregation or in the community who has led a small group in the past.

CHAPTER 5

At a Glance

1. Small Group Basics

- A small group consists of 4 to 12 people; 6 to 8 people are an ideal size.

- The purpose is to grow in faith and to grow closer to God as members minister to one another.

- God cares for people through people.

- All small groups are unique; no two are exactly alike.

- People join small groups in order to have their needs met.

- Meetings should last 60 to 90 minutes per session.

- Using prayer and the Bible makes a small group faith based.

- Take care in selecting a book. It can affect the quality of your discussions.

- Confidentiality is important. What is said in the group must stay within the group.

- What members receive from a small group is in direct proportion to their involvement in the group.

- Start meetings on time and end them on time.

2. Sample Format of a Small Group Meeting

- Social time (before the meeting starts).

- Check-in (members share what is new with them and how their week has been). Allow about 3 minutes per person.

- Announcements by the leader. Allow 5 minutes.

- Book discussion. Allow 25 to 30 minutes.

- Group activity. Allow about 20 minutes.

- Closing prayer with optional individual petitions. Allow 5 minutes.

- Refreshments and social time. Allow 10 to 15 minutes.

3. Top Ten Small Group "To Do" List

1. Focus on Christ. Jesus is the power of a faith-based small group.

2. Provide a nonthreatening supportive environment.

3. Be true to your objectives. Make some goals and strive to reach them.

4. Everyone should have a chance to participate in group discussions.

5. Encourage members to minister to one another.

6. The leader and participants need to be good listeners.

7. Remember that we all see things through different perspectives.

8. Love and accept group members just as they are.

9. Be honest. It is vital for members and the leader to be truthful.

10. If something isn't working, try something else. Feel free to experiment.

4. Top Ten Small Group "Don't" List

1. Don't isolate or leave anyone out.

2. Don't monopolize group discussions. Give all a chance to speak.

3. Don't skip a meeting. Each person adds life to a session.

4. Don't give up on a person or the group.

5. Don't expect perfection. People and groups are not perfect.

6. Don't have a closed mind. Be open to new people and new ideas.

7. Don't try to cover too much material in one session.

8. Don't be critical. Be supportive.

9. Don't be afraid to ask questions.

10. Don't ignore problems. Deal with them in a Christian way.

5. Top Ten Tips for Leaders for Good Discussions

1. Begin discussions by asking an open-ended general question.

2. Allow moments of silence.

3. Don't lecture.

4. Be interested in the opinions of others.

5. Prepare in advance. Read the chapter and think about the questions.

6. Practice being a good listener. Be attentive. Think about what is being said.

7. Have a few back-up questions in case some fall flat.

8. Be appreciative and supportive. Thank others for their ideas and participation.

9. Use passages from the Bible to add depth to discussions.

10. Remember that the success of a small group discussion depends on all the participants, not just the leader.